Still

MARY JO BALISTRERI

*To Dear Katy
with love,
Jo*

FUTURECYCLE PRESS
www.futurecycle.org

Cover artwork, "Tangerine with Leaf" by George Hodan; author photo by Frank Balistreri; cover and interior book design by Diane Kistner; Gentium Book Basic text with Cronos Pro titling

Library of Congress Control Number: 2018952393

Published by FutureCycle Press
Athens, Georgia, USA

ISBN 978-1-942371-58-8

Still /

adjective

not moving or making a sound
"the still body of the young man"

synonyms: motionless, unmoving, not moving a muscle, stock-still,
   immobile, inanimate, like a statue, as if turned to stone, rooted to the
   spot, transfixed, static, stationary

noun

deep silence and calm; stillness
"the still of the night"

synonyms: quietness, quiet, quietude, silence, stillness, hush, soundlessness

adverb

up to and including the present or the time mentioned; even now (or then)
   as formerly.
"he still lives with his mother"; "she's still running in circles"

synonyms: up to this time, up to the present time, until now, even now, yet

Dedicated to my granddaughters,
Brittany Elise and Abigail Nicole,
and as always to my dearest Frank.

Contents

blazing firewood...
we drink cider
with a bite

I

I Say *Yes*

Shimmering but cold, late afternoon rides
across day. Pushed by wind, the Gulf moves
fast but without ripples. And though the wind
negates the sun's warmth, it cannot erase
the diamond-dazzle or sheen of light
swallowing sailboats in its maw.
Gerard Manley Hopkins comes in on a wave—
on a wave his concept of inscape, living into
the thing, living into this blinding brightness,
entombed in its womb—saltwater sea,
amniotic fluid, floating cloud.
I cannot explain what's happening or the rise
of joy. But I say *Yes. Yes* to everything.

You've Never Seen Blue Like This

Ocean City, New Jersey, 2010

Standing on the threshold, light and salt air slow-dance;
coupling, a blur of silvery mist.

Quiet with dreams, daughters and granddaughters—
reluctant awakening, minimal conversation:

they fill coffee mugs, bowls of dry cereal; dawdle
from kitchen to pillowed chairs, the sofa; scrunch legs

underneath them or stretch out flat on the coffee table;
sluggish, they reach for books, notebooks,

like the light's unhurried path to us from the sun, the way
it eases into color—the sky's sheen, a diaphanous blue veil.

Can you imagine the romp up there? Blue's short wavelengths,
the bump against oxygen and nitrogen, spread of blue sparks,

and the distance they travel to cavort below, off the glass surface
of the ocean where they dive to the bottom, refract light from within?

Voices drift up from the beach, ozone-clean air, hint of brine and fish,
allure of chocolate—at last nudged into action, we scatter

like those reflective surfaces outside, bounce off each other;
talk of shells, cheesesteaks, tans.

Blue ocean—turquoise, sapphire, indigo as if a flame burned in its depths.
Saturated with the unretractable joy of light, we are mermaids in the sun.

Self-Portrait with Masks

Draw yourself, she said. *Pick a primary color.*
What is primary, I wondered as my first-grade
teacher handed out manila paper.

She gave instructions in red, yellow, and blue.
I chose the yellow crayon, the yellow of buttercups,
the *gold drops* Dad called Mother's curls.

I chose it for the window shades in my bedroom
when tagged by a breeze, when motes
of yellow-beige fairy dust billowed around me.

I was a yellow girl.

But the yellow disappeared on the manila paper.
I shaded it with red to call attention to its leaving.
Red left with yellow and turned my image orange.

The orange of sunset, the orange of signs.
What happened to the yellow of me?
I outlined myself in black, made my yellow dress blue.

My dress turned green.
How slippery it was to make a portrait.

I held my picture up for the class.
The teacher praised the bold black,
the ruddy orange of my hair, my emerald green dress.

Enthused, I made other portraits. Added mauve,
chartreuse, hot pink, colors that were new to me.

I came to bask in the art of masks.
Later, I realized that praise had replaced
my original color.

Dear Vincent,

*They say—and I am very willing to believe it—that it is difficult to know
yourself, but it isn't easy to paint yourself either.*
—Vincent Van Gogh

Your *Self-Portrait with Straw Hat* looks at me
from across the kitchen table. You look like I feel. It's why your eyes
hold me, I suppose—the questions, hurt and disappointment.
But I don't have your animal eyes—alert, ready to attack.

It is not color that torments and delights me, but sound.
Since I lost my hearing, a tune plays perpetually in my head.
Sometimes I just want the music to stop. It can't or won't.
I feel as if I too might go crazy,
as if this ceaseless spiral will consume me.

It's not so much your likeness that interests me but how
you painted your fire—all that intensity discharging at once,
the frenzy of chaos, how you gave voice to it, ordered it.

Art historians talk more about color theory and the impact of Seurat
in this painting which is all here. But I'm wondering if you and I
have the same pressure—something we love so insistent in our head.

You handled it with a paintbrush. I try to write. We partner
in a risky dance with fragmentation—will we lose ourselves
in the attempt to honor excessive noise
attempting to calm and extract what we need?

With your strong ego, you quell fear and aggression
on the canvas with the yellows of your straw hat, your eyes.

I wrangle with music through words, but at a slower pace—
black on white like the keyboard I once played.

I feel your canvas throb with color's dynamic, imagine
the implosion in your head unraveling down your arm,

the often-manic obsession to get it down,
executing the impossible through fervor and persistence.
A portrait that's true can be wrung inside out.

You give hope by showing anguish
behind the surface; even your demons
were made to serve art.

Losing Language

The dog next door barks and barks.
My husband shakes me.
You're dreaming, he says, but even now I see the dogs
upon me, gripping scraps of paper between their teeth,
water-stained words, blurred phrases, torn pages.
Each time a thought appears, a dark-haired woman
raises a stop sign, cuts me with contempt—
Not important, too small. Not good enough.
Something is missing I'll never get back. Water pours
from the faucet I can't reach, and slides over
the bathtub rim. I shudder in the black surge, alarms
screeching in my ears, words even now sinking
to the bottom. Dark heads of dogs swim closer, barking.
It's just a dream, my husband says again.
I sit up on the bed. Shaken. Relieved.
I know what I know. I tell my husband
I'll be but a minute—walk to my desk,
and retrieve the yellow legal pad:
The dog barks and barks. My husband shakes me.

Regret Nothing

The days you didn't keep promises to yourself
    your hothouse vocabulary flourished
      tension nibbled away words and silence became stasis

The tomes you wrote on escape
    the marriage
    Wisconsin
    the dead-end cold

The sterile days of winter in the bone
    mahogany gloom and children dying

The sour taste of loneliness and depression
    unanswered phone calls and missed meetings
    skipped classes and the memorial...

Listen instead to *Variations on a Theme* by Paganini
Allow the trembling vibration as bow reaches blood and bone
Gaze out the window
Let your eyes rest where the red of winter wheat
    flames in a prairie you thought bare

Woman Wrapped in Orange

There is no yellow or no blue without orange.
—Vincent Van Gogh

She is a Hermès bag, voluptuous in orange,
an orange-shaded tiger on a bottle of merlot,
the sepals of a hibiscus. She is mangrove
leaf soaked in the sun, and California poppy
that sashays when she moves.

Gumball-bright and bold *Moon over Miami,*
a juicy orange Honey Bell, this girl is presence,
a slice of orange surfing in the dark blue Atlantic,
an orange prop-plane trailing advertisements.

Occasionally she's a sharp cheddar or a hot curry,
a prickly pear or a habanero, but mostly a monarch,
an orange free state *unto herself.*

Alone at home, she releases the orange helium
balloon of herself, kicks off the electric orange Zappos
and hangs the Hermès bag.
She fixes a fresh-squeezed screwdriver and unwinds.
In her chair by the window, the crunch of carrots
satisfies. She sips the drink, watches sunset.

As the room turns blood orange, bittersweet,
and burnt, she curls up in the chair,
golden orange and translucence, sweet release
into the sealed amber of the night.

Veterans Day

The first snow of the year
falls steadily
the world outside the window
at peace
Bronzed leaves hang at the sides
of shagbark hickories
mute witnesses
to season's end

In the dirge of snow's adagio
men and women lie under snow
somewhere at rest

The white flakes drift
in this gray sky
star-shaped and falling
on Iraqi fields
falling on the snow-capped mountains
of Afghanistan

The last sunflower in the barrel
closed its petals this morning
ragged cloak faded
though it braved frost
and freezing rain for months

Maybe

the fabric of life
unravels
because the weave
seeks a new design

Maybe

wordless is the red light
of tangled thoughts
tiny knots
in the knit and purl of life

Maybe

a blank page
the white solitude needed
to clear one's mind
and imagine a new stitch

Rebooting

On the way to the pond, braced against the cold,
I hear my father:
Take a long deep breath. Take it inside you.

I inhale marsh and musk.
The plonk of a carp emphasizes the silence.
A crow caws from the oak.

When I was a child, I listened for geese.
When they roosted, their raucous voices delighted,
their chatter my bedtime lullaby.

Strange how as time collapses, it expands.
Without a ticking clock, the click of a computer,
iPhone, and iPad, time proves seamless.

A squirrel scamps through underbrush.
An orange canoe holds winter light.
Crystallized grasses tick.

As if hearing these sounds for the first time,
something like delight billows inside—
such abundant life within this stillness.

All these months, shuttered tight against
anything impinging on my work—and for what?
I've become absent from myself.

Standing, my face lifted to the cold,
breath creates a soft mist like wisps of smoke.
The air smells green.

II

Transitions

Golden leaves baked crisp
steeped in the sky's fragrance

Pumpkins dotting brittle fields
with orange globes of sun

The pond's stone-cold mirror
rebuffing reflection

A white linen tablecloth
to cover the brittle stubble of wheat

Burnished clouds spilling
over the vast vase of earth

Elongated Nordic-blue shadows
crawling out from sprigs of scarlet sumac

All this to celebrate
before the seamless skein of winter

In the Days When Wood Was Unaffordable

We placed red candles on black-painted bricks
in the fireplace, flames in staggered pinpoints,
our stars in the night.

The children asleep, we sat on the old Naugahyde sofa,
listened to our first stereo. Night after night we leaned
into Suzanne's mystery sung by Leonard Cohen,
with *tea and oranges that come all the way from China,*

our minds striving toward the verdigris Lady as boats slipped
into New York harbor, grasped by what we could not grasp,
the promise, the distant light.

Today, a day of heat and aqua sea, different harbor, different boats,
an orange on my plate. The memory of that time comes to me
with winter and the warmth of Cohen's music,
the words we tried to travel by.
Your brokenness. Mine.

And the sun pours down like honey while a pileated woodpecker
hammers the tree, and you are here from your dead distance,
and though nothing's the same, my love,
I am the same, still here,
still listening.

Skipping Stones in Ireland

The boy wades into the shallows, pants rolled to his knees,
the back of his body sculpted in light and shade.

In contrapposto, he calls across time, and I see
the Greek *Discus Thrower,* that ease and expertise.

With shoulders slanted to the universe, he twists
on his own axis, movement barely perceptible.

Only the voice of the skipping stone, its ripples and eddies
across the surface of the River Liffey breaks the quiet.

But, for now, what moves me most is not his muscled beauty
or intense focus, but the knowing he holds within

to make a stone walk on water.

Winter at a Beachfront Restaurant

I watch ten-year-old girls explode into waves.
Their white eyelet dresses flutter like the feathers
of gulls that gyrate over them in the falling light.
Bronze-skinned boys run back and forth on the beach.
Young laughter hovers around my chair
through screenless windows in this late afternoon.

On the pier, fishermen cast graceful arcs
to a turquoise Gulf. I follow the curve of one silver line
when it snaps, collapses, jars lose a memory
of Lake Superior, five-year-old Billy.
Disappearing into the indigo water.

I barely hear the man sweeping sand from under my table,
try to fix on the glistening backs of boys carrying beach chairs,
chaise lounges, and bright blue umbrellas.
Sand castles begin to crumble.
I can almost hear the wail of the Aerial Bridge,
the three-blast horn signal from the iron ore ship.
And, always, the scream that still screams
as undertow swallows his red shirttail.
No-see-ums begin to bite,
something that stings
            long after they're gone.

Boating on the Yerres

Men lift the sky
    in a shower of veiled hues, wooden paddles
dipping deep in the liquid silk of the Yerres.

    With rippled strokes, they guide their skiffs,
slip silently between rows of poplars.
    A woman watches from the sanatorium, sees
trees shimmy in the skimmed wakes.

The green sheen of reeds begins to sweep her mind
    clean of all but the light, the men and the charmeuse
skein of river becoming shadows in the sun-drunk air.

Closing her eyes, she drinks the breeze, the stillness
    of this country afternoon, the lap of water on hull
as soothing as a lullaby.
    Shifts of color and luminosity flicker behind her eyelids.

In the cradle of her boat, she is alive to each vibration,
    braided into the melody of river music.

Ripple

1.

Sun bakes early afternoon into stillness.
    I tuck myself into a corner of the sofa,
        a moist cloth over my eyes.

We'd had a lecture in the morning on Picasso,
    and one question kept repeating itself—

Who sees the human face correctly?
    Is it the photographer, the mirror, or the painter?

Just last week, my husband's ex-wife told the children
    to call me *dogface.*

The smallest child reveals the name in dinner table talk,
    saying, *You don't look like a dog.*
        The teenager smirks.
            Look in the mirror, my husband says.
            You're not a dog.

2.

On a morning walk, the tide is a shallow sucking sound.
    Dogface was a joke until I sent the older child
        to her room. *Dogface, dogface,* she screamed.

Rise above it, my husband says. *Others have had worse fates.*
    Picasso's Dora comes to mind. He painted his feelings—
        Dora with shark teeth and a big mouth.

Forget Picasso, the question, the ex-wife—What does it matter?
    Suddenly a mussel shell pricks my foot—the beach
        is littered with them. I kick them out of the way,

furious at the beach, the ex-wife, myself, and most of all my husband.
    Who is he to tell me to rise above it?
        Why doesn't he reprimand his own kids?

Dark schools of stingrays float beneath the glazed opaque surface
of the Gulf. They don't look like their relative, the shark,
but each carries more than one barbed stinger.

Low gray clouds begin to mass on the horizon. Out at sea,
a pelican plummets into the unguarded immensity.
One ripple spread ever wider.

Unveiled

Sunset, and carp leap to where the sky dips its wings,
widening rings moving out to estuary's edge, last light
disappearing even as it swells.

Darkness deepens. A woman sits outside in her willow rocker
inhaling night's subtle heat, heavy with humidity. She sips
burgundy. A great horned owl amplifies stillness.

Whoo-Whoo winds through forests of mangrove, shape-shifts
in her head. *Who-Who are you?*
In the shadowed ebony of water and trees, she isn't sure.

Words, once come easily, have disappeared. She imagines
herself tromping through marsh grass and mudflats,
alligators slithering under water, hoarse croak of egrets.

Quiet.... Darkness swallows and mutes the owl's barely audible voice.
Air holds the dampness of foliage, roots, faint smell of mold.
The wine warms; rocking soothes.

She's becoming what enters her, the rhythm of her own
movement, the anchor that holds,
riding in on the breath that transports her back to self.

Loggerhead

Belly-up on sand
a position I've never seen

Three of us
roll her over

Empty sockets—
vultures have eaten both eyes

Barnacles scab her great domed shell
tangles of seaweed   clumps of mud

Water wind-whipped
sea-cold spindrift

Something tumbles between us

On the Fourteenth Anniversary of Her Death

for my mother

In her last six months, she sipped chamomile tea
    while Nat King Cole sang

Mostly silence filled her as June turned into December
    and dusk's matte shadows expanded along the ground

Blades of bone protruded through her thin apricot sweater
    and some days were one long nap

The more she lost   the more she gave away
        watercolors   copper enamels
      handmade quilts   tap shoes and original routines

Tonight, feathered wings brush across the sky
    wisps of purple-peach
        layered like the colors she painted on canvas

There is nowhere I go she isn't

Heron

in the spongy crush of duckweed
    in the season's moist swelling
a heron stands within
a strand of cattails and reeds
    reflecting
    leaning not
    toward emptiness
but jungle-lust desire

Migration of Sandhill Cranes along the Platte River

Into the mutable colors of dusk, bugles of thousands
    wrest open the sky. Crisscross of flight after flight.
        A horizon of extended necks and stretched-out legs.

The gray shape-shifting mass dissolves, separates, unites,
    wings rattle the air, multitudes call back and forth—
        family to family, parent to child. They rend

and mend the skyways, trumpet choruses that bind like an invisible thread,
    the sound of millions of years stitching one generation to the next.
        Into the flap and flutter of deepening twilight

we follow the grand convocation, a spectacle of
    crimson crowns, tumultuous explosion of cries,
        wings flicking just slightly upward before

graceful, gangly legs drop down into courtships of bows and leaps,
    jumps and pirouettes. They throw back their heads; they bounce.
        The chicks imitate the acrobatic dance of parents. In awe

we watch skein upon skein of returning cranes come here to roost,
    to stand one-legged throughout the night,
        recreating the Platte and prairie into cranes
          as far as the eye can see.

III

Praise

the sawgrass ripening
and cattail wands
an eagle's keen over mangroves
and spoonbills mining mudflats

a lone kite   angled and aloft
vultures that drape the sky
osprey fishing from ribboned nests

Praise the angler's wicker creel
white caps that riff the waves
tide edging up pylons on the pier

trellises of trumpet vines
bamboo clacking in the wind
the thin blue cast
of a skimmed milk sky

Praise this day that beckons
scoops me into its net
this spacious silence
this joy that is morning

Mademoiselle Boissière Knitting

Portrait of Mademoiselle Boissière Knitting
—Gustave Caillebotte, oil on canvas, 1877

In stillness she is the sound of dusk washing ashore,
the fading silence in music.

Jammed between the affluent layers
of a rich Parisian family—a room crowded
with ormolued mahogany, ripe with vine
and flowered surroundings, she acknowledges
but does not succumb to old age diminishment.

She sits at her work table, bends to her task.
In plum dress and bonnet, glasses slipped down
on her nose, mouth pouty with concentration,
she transforms white wool, makes imagination
concrete, strikes a bright light against her dark dress.

Though everything in the room tends to engulf her,
she holds her ground. *Do not toy with me* could be
a placard announcing her intention, her needle
sharp as a sword.

She knits and purls, unspools herself like the yarn,
exudes a quiet, sustained energy
in the continuous process of precise moments.

Like the sea at sunset, she reminds me of edges,
advance and retreat of tides, the porous
borders of our lives,
how the dead come from the living.

At day's end the moon begins to rise; stars appear.
In Mademoiselle's end there is nothing
but endless beginning.

At 38 Weeks

I carried your dead body
inside me for ten days.
No one suspected you had died.
The nursery waited in yellow and blue.
Your siblings were wild with excitement.
Piano students arrived on schedule.
Only at night, alone with my thoughts,
did I pray for a reprieve—
some mistaken reading of the ultrasound.
I dreamed of your possibility.

On September 14, I paced back and forth
in the lobby of the courthouse, your father
inside wrangling over some old issue.
Though dead, my body labored for your birth,
pushed you down the dark passage.
We crouched in that lobby,
waiting for the scales of justice to be balanced.
Silence too, weighed in.

Stillborn

Afterward, I never saw you again.
An unmarked box. An unmarked common grave.
Forgive us. We had no money.

They gave us your birth certificate.
We inscribed your name, Daniel Joseph.
You were clothed with love.

I remember your high cheekbones, shock
of black hair. It was your father's.
He's gone now, too.

The Boys We Carried

Neither of us is prepared for the curve in conversation.
As my friend struggles with words, her story begins
to emerge, a story just like mine from twenty years ago.

Neither of us ever asked, or knew we could ask,
why our bodies betrayed us,
how our full-term babies died inside of us.

Quietness was deemed normal.
They were small with softer heartbeats.
Why were the doctors unconcerned—until it was too late?

Fissures open. We say our boys' names almost
shyly. Swapping stories, we begin
to interrupt each other.

>   Andrew comes to me when I'm doing laundry,
>   sometimes in the garden.
>   Danny visits when I'm making dinner or at the pond.

Both our boys like quiet and often appear at night.

We walk toward the exit, arms around each other's waist.
Halfway out the door, my friend stops—
Maybe we were the dead ones.

The screen bangs behind us.

Without a Voice

Akhmatova in the prison queues in Leningrad.
Tillie Olsen at the ironing board—
her writing in storage.

Beyond color and creed, across country and continent,
a war of intimidation continues to pound at every door.
Each story different, each story the same. They all bleed
across the pages of our lives—the sound of a bullet
shattering Malala's face, the brain of Gabrielle Giffords.

Head shots of women cascade through history,
screams often stifled by their own hands.
More often though, the hand that stills is a man's—
pressure from his finger closing her lips.
Afraid, she casts her eyes down,
hardens herself to marble.

The women's faces float
across our unconscious in dreams,
flash across the television.
The loss of their voices a burden so heavy
we stumble under the weight.

At what point in speaking
the language of silence
do we become a quarry of stone?

In the Parking Lot of the Hardware Store

a stray dog meanders
shadow of white fur

a woman sits in a heated car
waits for her husband

tendrils of fog   a confusing semaphore
ghostly men carrying propane tanks
buckets of paint
burlap bags of birdseed

the woman's eyes tear
her mouth tightens
she craves salt eats a pretzel

writes in her notebook
I've mistaken this life for my own

the stray crouches beneath her car

Charade

Faux leather bag slung over her shoulder,
the *Times* under her arm,
heels tapping on pavement,
she walks into the soft morning light
of a neighborhood café.

Taking a side table, she orders French roast,
a bran muffin. Skims headlines.
She really likes a place with lamps,

a place small and intimate where women
in tennis skirts come to replay their game.
Others chit-chat while they knit,
clicking needles soothing in the background.

She likes the snippets of conversation
that purl around her as she sips, as she holds
the cup to her cheek, feeling
the emotional well-being that must spring
from childhood.

Sometimes one of the women will stop,
compliment her dress, her scarf.

She toys with crumbs from the muffin,
glances at the time. She'll tell them if they ask
where she's headed—*To the office,*
but first my morning fix.
They'll laugh with her, understand how it is.

Afterward she'll walk back home,
change into sweats.
Pore over the want ads.

Gabriele Münter Paints Her Lover

after *Boating,* oil on canvas, 1910, Milwaukee Art Museum

For days I live in the landscape of our lives,
painting our story against your gathering darkness.
On canvas, bristles in yellow sulfur ignite the sky.
Though I am lake to your mountain, heart to your mind,
you stand apart, lofty and aloof.
I paint you that way in the boat.

That afternoon, I pushed my body into the oars, plunged them
into water to divert the undertow's force, a potency
I pulled back into my hands, up through my arms and thighs.
Waves crested and fell: How I worshipped you,
knelt at your feet, an awe-struck student. Loving you was easy.

Now you see yourself as a god—but do not underestimate me.
I will not lose my way this time.
Equal in art, I steady you like the base of a triangle.
I am ballast to your sail.

Your words swish against the side of our boat,
but my desires penetrate the canvas—
cerulean and sapphire, softest blue of morning.

I am maker of deep green peace, creator of mountains
saturated in royal blue. The sky is mine,
complex and swirling, brushed with the lightest touch.

Discovering My Mother in a Painting
by Mary Cassatt

She catches me with her half-smile,
unconscious delight flowering over her.
I finger the single strand around my neck,
eyes fixed on the woman with pearls—my pearls, my mother's.

It may be the pastel color lit by lamps of rosy hue
as she looks out from her balcony, or maybe it's the sheen
of her strawberry-blonde hair curled back behind her ear
that mesmerizes and transports me
to the theaters of my mother's dancing career:
the chandelier casting soft reflections, the rustle
of anticipation in the upper tiers before lights dim.

I remember her Irish skin—milk-white porcelain, the blush
that tinted her cheeks. Any minute she might break
out in that hearty laugh, infectious to anyone around her.
Even in the wake of dying, light glints off her coral scarf
and nightgown like the leaps and pliés of her life.

I long for my mother, on loan from somewhere else,
who's stopped to linger here for a spell
in the Art Institute. Too soon she'll have to leave again,
but here, where shadows are part of light,
is where I stand.

Along the Fox River

A woman comes to the river. Stands silent.
Absorbed in the billowing shapes and soundings
of a daughter's life, having navigated the dangerous shoals
of memory, her attention drifts to migrating crows
wheeling across the sky. She holds out her hands
for whirligigs—how easily they spiral from their source.
In the waning light, beech trees along the river
morph into pillars of a faraway temple.
She imagines chimes, a hundred chimes. Color
becomes sound, echoes off stone, splinters the air.
The heavier grasses of summer, winnowed of hue,
turn into ethereal fields of fireflies.
In the humidity-thick night they signal for mates,
their blinking lanterns like earth stars.

How to Deal with the Dead

Do you think by constant partying you'll be too busy
to miss them? When they finally get you alone,
they will knock you flat with presence. Stay home
and converse where it's comfortable. Their dialect
is strange, but possible to understand.

Talk about them to others. They love the sound
of their own name, just as you do.
Just because you can't see
them doesn't mean they aren't there.

Visit the gravesites. Their spirits hover there
and it's a good place to have some fun.
Once at Sam's grave, an orange Cheshire cat
balloon broke away and flew up to the tallest tree
right above us. We looked up at that grinning face.
You had to laugh. That was a Sam kind of joke.

Expect to feel a roller coaster of emotion. Intensity.
Numbness isn't rare. A flood of tears after coming upon
that chocolate chip cookie mix in the grocery is common.
Despair and lethargy creep up like kudzu. Curse.
The dead are used to cursing. It brings unabated release.

Treat them in death like they were in life. Most of them
are like you. The cliché *Don't gild the lily* is good
to remember. Zach, for example, smeared peanut butter on
doorknobs for April Fool's, removed his older sister's clothes
from her closet and recorded her yelling. When he died,
we weren't surprised that his last bed was made
like a shiny black Bat Mobile. That was pure Zach.

Wear bright colors. Celebrate their lives. The dead rejoice
in outrageous oranges, purples, big gold hoop earrings.

My mom wore chunky turquoise beads and she always comments
when I wear them. She was a painter. We did *Color Me Beautiful*
together. She still speaks in color. Sam, too.
Today, I wear an orange ring that he's crazy about.

Without a body, the dead have freedom to go anywhere.
My mom showed up once as a daisy
blooming all by herself in a wooded area,
and it wasn't even summer.
How impossible is that!
She was always good for surprises, and besides she knew how
fabulous she looked in her petaled dress.

They like lots of attention, same as us. And they are adept
communicators. Sometimes they use signs. Sometimes emotion.
The five senses. Last night at the symphony, I was moved
by the joy in the music and Grandpa must have been too. He sat
in the empty seat next to me. I could hear his relief when he said,
I wondered how long it would take you to see merit in Mahler.

Rather than curl up into absence, take a walk, talk with a friend.
This *oneness thing* does not bring them closer. The dead are
fiercely independent. Give them room to breathe.

IV

Late December Sun

late December sun
its light touch
on ancient ridged trees

branches of willows
anchored in ice
perches for sparrows and chickadees

falling flakes that drift
in silence
in peace

oaks' bronzy leaves
waving in wind lend sepia shadows
to winter's seamless whitened fields

frosted window panes
spangles of dreamscapes
like antique lace

aged trees burning
in our hearths
kindling even the coldest heart

the solstice
candling the dark
this shortest day
this new beginning

Let Us Praise Gray

for its ease into morning—
enfolding the night while
unrolling the day—
the color that issues forth the landscape—
where shape evolves into mangroves,
a gray heron waking,
the roosting egret and sharp-shinned hawk.
Where sun paints the sea's first base coat
before myriad layers in shades of blue.

For its quiet accord, let us praise gray. *No color
but nuance,* said Paul Verlaine. Painters choose
gray, for gray never fights;
blended with white, it is satin and silver,
the graceful gowns that glow in Dutch paintings.
Blended with black, dark mysteries of Rembrandt,
gradations of shadows to luminous light.
And let us commend gray, its ultimate soulfulness,
the monochrome palettes of Whistler, Picasso,
the wide range of hue from mother to war.

Let us bless gray for the clouds' black play,
the silver-gray splay of light after storms,
of mountains grayed and flattened by haze
or fingers of smoke, their charcoal smudge,

mist over water, the rain and snow,
dew in clear globes on the swelling bud,
the skies of feathers and ostrich plumes.

For its calm simplicity, let us praise gray,
its homespun humility, neutrality, composure.
Gray, most stable, least pushy, reflective,
the color that welcomes, says *come,* says *stay.*

1929

They crashed with the stock market on a Friday.
When the bank failed, he was credited with a trunk
of paper promises. He forfeited himself.
After a nervous breakdown, relief was a jug of wine.
What she brought home kept the house
around them. She peddled beauty and hope
from door to door. Housewives who struggled
opened themselves to her. They had their ways—
envelopes marked rent, grocer, utilities,
and always one unmarked. What harm, a tinge of rouge,
a new red lipstick, that soft face powder?
Her products helped them cope; their purchases
helped her stave off starvation.
Women, the dabs of color in a world turned gray.

How Light Casts Its Net

for Ruth Conklin

Remember the orange summer of flowers, gardens
that opened onto chrysanthemums as we sauntered
along the avenue, iced mochas in hand, looking for bargains
the rush of autumn left behind?

Remember the black sleeveless dress you bought that day
marked down to a ridiculously low price? The way you twirled
in a full skirt, black sash tied in front?
As *light as a breeze,* you said.

And now a breathless day in October, sun burning
on your bare arms, you stand in another kind of garden,
hem of that same black dress barely moving.
The white heat intensifies. Steeple bells peal the hour.

The priest empties your husband's cremains, scatters them
like a path in the rich, dark soil. You look down,
shards of bone too bright in the glare. Your hand plucks
at the skirt's cotton fabric. It clings to your skin in the heat.

Backpacking in North Central Wisconsin

Off the trail, we stumble across a smorgasbord
of scorched leftovers, shards of glass, dented Buds.

A murder of crows scolds as we shuffle through debris
tainted with rot, acrid accumulation of empty tuna tins,
cigarette butts, a dead squirrel, a Monopoly board
chewed at Broadway, remnants of a charcoaled O'Keeffe print,
Golden Books almost beyond recognition.

We try to ignore the crows' continuous cacophony. We focus
instead on charred pines, the buckled roof, fallen chimney stones.

What do you think happened, I ask my husband.
He offers lightning, careless hikers, something gone wrong
with the pot-bellied stove.

I envision a family at their kitchen table passing out paper money,
plastic houses, hotels, a mother reading "The Three Bears,"
children huddled at her knees.

Sometimes, my husband says, *what one loves, one can also destroy.*
His words linger.

Wind soughs through the evergreens.
A black feather flutters down.

Snapshot, Late Winter, 1997

Don't let it be forgot, that once there was a spot...
—Alan Jay Lerner and Frederick Loewe

A crystallized Scottie, tail in air, crouches
beside a smiling snow family in front of the house,
a group portrait before they disappear. Tufts of brown grass
have begun to squeeze through the melt.

Snow Mother wears an apron and red hat. Her pine-branch arm
curls around a rake. Papa, attired in a felt fedora, has a red chain
around his neck. The child, red-scarfed with a knit hat,
grips the red rope of an empty Country Squire wagon.

The snapshot lies under amber glass on my desk,
a story we have not yet imagined,
something in the distance we cannot see:
the boy dead, his mother dying, the father absent,
our family ephemeral as snow—even then.

Tomorrow You Go Up in Smoke

You said it might be good to go down in the pinstripe,
the Miró tie, its surrealist fish.
We talked about outfitting you like a Pharaoh—
the long-stemmed cherrywood pipe,
a pouch of *No Bite Delight,*

both of us in hysterics over the aroma of chocolate
and caramel overtones wafting from the coffin.
We took turns adding items—your carved cane
from Yellowstone, the fraternity paddle,
your two best architectural models.
Yeats and Stevens.

You'd wear your glasses, your class ring. Strange
we never bought wedding bands.
Now I wish we had.

A sense of *last time* catches in my throat.
Alive yesterday. Forever's emptiness today.
How do I get my mind around *forever?*

What You Left Me

Sheer peach drapes sag in the sun's wide eye
vacuum silent and uncoiled on the beige carpet

grandfather clock from your childhood stopped at 8:02—
chimes useless as time

oatmeal-raisin cookies hard as stones in glass cashew jar
coffee pot unplugged

black karaoke case on the counter
Willie Nelson's "Red-Headed Stranger" hanging out its sleeve

dress shoes waiting by the door
beveled mirror in the foyer

splotches of dried blood on the white marble floor
your eyes as mine

blue, startled

Angel Flying Too Close to the Ground

Today he gets a flu shot. Picks up a sliver
in his finger at the clinic. He's angry
at the nurse for taking too much blood.
    A person only has so much.

He washes a few dishes in a sink heavy with suds,
flash of his yellow gloves in and out of bubbles
like a canary at its bath. He takes this chore seriously,
does not notice or care that water runs
down the cabinets and splashes onto the floor.

Risen from the dead of a subdural hematoma, he is
a handful, this eighty-nine-year-old father.
Shiny-eyed with the unexpected gift of second sight,
he craves independence, dislikes being
questioned, becomes cagey and stubborn, and moves
beyond the ability of unused legs teetering toward disaster.

In the slant of late afternoon sun, I sit at the table
and ponder the turn of events. I think of Martha and Mary,
wonder how they coped with Lazarus newly emerged
from the tomb. Were they, too, stunned into disbelief
that he had come back the same, but somehow different?

Evening, and he curls up in his lounge chair, dinner napkin clutched
in his hand like a small stuffed animal. Willie Nelson sings
in the background; his closed eyelids flutter like wings.
On a night like this did Mary sigh, look upon her brother
like I look upon my father, and say to Martha,
    Look how tender, how soundly he sleeps.

Shifting Sands at Bonita Beach

At lowest tide, moon spectral in the sky,
hundreds of shells rise through the sand.

What's happening? I ask an old man.

Nothing, he says, fishing pole over his shoulder.
They're whelks trying to burrow to safety, escape the birds.

By the dunes, waves crest and collapse.
Empty shells litter the beach. I lift one,
turn it over. Like my father's house,
it echoes with silence—
my father, who doesn't recognize my face.

Sometimes he hums snatches of songs,
but he has lost the key,
his shadowed smile uncertain.

White foam becomes dark sand,
the tideline no more real than the horizon.
For the whelk, daylight is often death
whereas life flourishes under the sea.

Maybe my father has entered shadow,
the sun-warmed shelter of his life.

He seems happy.
Perhaps lack of language
is something other than loss.

In the Shortened Days of December

Dad trudges along a worn trail, cups his ear,
listening:
a small wind,
a bird chirping among the evergreens,
ice cracking at the edge of a pond.

Each day he withdraws by fractions,
the shadow of his past gaining flesh.

By late afternoon, he abandons the trail
for his recliner where sun strokes his face
and he leaves
for the early years of the century at Curley's Bar.

In his dreaming, he sings as he always did,
*blue skies smiling above...*his voice traveling
through the dim interior, the smoke-crowded room,
winding its way to the door that's opened—and the light
that momentarily haloes Mary, sweetheart and wife

in her straw picture hat, who crosses the threshold,
standing for a moment in amber.

All There's Left to Say

When the scent of wild strawberries wafts from the woods
and returns the juicy-sweet meadows of childhood,
when the double pleasure of present and past throws me
this heady bouquet
on a day already fully flowered with gifts,

I praise.

While on the cedar boardwalk through the mangrove forest,
when glossy green leaves reach out,
when tangled and twisted prop roots snare imagination's
strange wildness and warblers, unseen, call out in song,

I praise.

And when at last the calm pond of the Gulf stretches
blue beyond the horizon and sews itself seamlessly to the sky,
when it lifts the edge of its white-skirted flounce to the sand,

what can I do but praise

and praise again

as thousands of filmy wings flit backward, forward, hover
their last hurrahs, their last two weeks in the air
after a lifetime of water—
these dragonflies, damsels, their new resplendence
mating, creating—Oh joyous affirmation of life—

Praise and praise and praise.

Waiting for the Light Rail

She sits in an alcove of light and dark,
a pause between coming and going.
She's an empty bench, a blank sheet of paper,
a sign askew, a mouthful of air,
a pencil in hand, and the *now of now.*
In the spaciousness of release, her mind fills
with words; the words become flesh,
and a cement shelter melds with the loam
of a thousand fields, fragrant as the fleshy blooms
that dangled from her father's pear trees. Now, on the cusp
of summer, the wind ruffles her hair, rustles leaves
she cannot see, carries the whistle of the oncoming train—
is the breath that writes the living poem,
intertwined, inexhaustible.

Improv on Blue

Hunched over the keyboard, lost
in a blue translation of sound, his fingers fly
in chromatic parallels of motion, become tone
clusters, augmented wave-breakers, blocks
of color—midnight blue, teal and turquoise—
and suddenly he stands,
bends over the piano's harp, plucks strings
in the sea of a smoke-blue room
where he unlooses
violet-backed starlings, iridescent
in drained glassware
and upturned spoons,
soft as a handkerchief floating to the floor;
and then, as he sits down, left hand pounding like a stiff wind,
right blurring the black notes, he modulates
to G minor and a riff on Goldberg variation 21, indigo
bursting in contrapuntal rhythms, dropping between stars;
and now he mutters the inexpressible,
circles in diminished fifths, only to find himself
in Sainte-Chapelle, Paris,
a Bach Unaccompanied Cello Suite inundating his mind,
hollow footsteps on the cobbles after the concert
until he awakens with a start,
the crowd wild,
and he, triumphant in blue.

I Believe

after Linda Pastan

we married for all the wrong reasons. Apart
for twenty-eight years, our lives were happy
enough except for the one thing we were denied.
Each other.

I believe
    we married because the day
    you asked me, the sun sifted down memories
    that flickered into bloom,
    love had no past tense,
    and the pounding roar of the sea muted all
    but desire.

I believe
    you carried my unlived life,
    that you were still sixteen with tasseled
    loafers, a dark and handsome extrovert
    with a vintage green Ford;

    that I froze you in time, as you did me, the girl
    with the blonde pageboy, the girl next door who played the piano.

I came to believe
    you were Handel's *Water Music,* beautiful in large
    spaces, a loner who was also addicted to work.
    You came to believe I had never been the girl next door.

I believe
    on our twentieth anniversary that learning to dance
    made a difference as we moved from the tango to the waltz,
    became content with the two-step before we mellowed
    into the stroll,

    and that, in the dance of life, in the *yes* of free will, in the *yes* of destiny,
    I came to believe in us.

Rocky III

Even with the door partially closed
I hear the man I love
    heavy-tread
    steady back and forth
    pacing silence

Snarled by quiet   I look through the crack
    shoulders slouched over desk
    eyes buried in the abyss of the ledger
    pencil pressing   erasing
    fingers punching

When the plaintive folk-like theme of Rachmaninoff's
    third piano concerto begins   I know the music
will minister as I cannot   Words do not help
Intimacy does not bring him closer
When we first married   I did not understand this need
    to find the distance of himself
    did not know that only by his leaving   could he return

I peel potatoes for dinner   long brown curls of melodic line
    warm water removing surface dirt
I put them in a pot of boiling water   the furious third movement
reaches a climax   opens space for howl and rage
steam of illusion and grief   until spent
    he can let go and I can mash and mash

In the Kitchen with My Husband

with a nod to Tony Hoagland

Perhaps I exaggerated
when I called my husband
a Neanderthal.

But some days, when he comes
from his basement office,
I still think *cave.*

I came from the East Coast
to what I considered the wilderness of Wisconsin.
Was long-distance love a mistake?

I didn't really mean primitive—
maybe unyielding.
I seldom got a thought for my penny.

An examined life is not worth living, he'd say.
You must be joking, I'd say.
No, not at all, his reply.

This linear thinker kept the underpinnings
of our house in stellar condition, bird feeders full,
the grass mowed.

He also brought me coffee in bed
with the morning paper. Sometimes
he'd come home with yellow roses.

Today we stand at either end of the center island,
separate butcher blocks.
I make salad.
He marinates meat.

Renoir Paints My Husband and Me at Breakfast in Cagnes-Sur-Mer

To let the world know after our time that we were here,
and that we loved.

—Renoir

My husband marvels at the artist's accomplishment,
his brush fat with alizarin crimson, adding a touch
of pigment to the apples. The still-life of our table:
linens scented with sun, their creases, violet-hued
white plates and cups, a pitcher of *café au lait,*
frothy foam spilling from dark roast,
two rustic Chanticleer apples sweet and ripe,
warm in chrome yellow, smoky glaze of red-blue,
redolent of earth's loamy richness.

I pour the *café,* pass the wicker basket
of *pains aux chocolat* studded with nuggets of cocoa butter,
flaky layers of pastry where my love, a smile on his face,
still leans toward me these many years,

this warm September where even now
the sky doubles itself in the Bay d'Antibes, and he dabs
at the goodness dribbling down my chin,
my eyes closed to the sun.

At a Writers Retreat in the North Woods of Wisconsin

A heron
braided in reeds and cattails
scans the lake
bides his time

A school of minnows
swims south in the pond
aware too late
of the heron's spear-sharp beak

Hunger quenched
the blue-shaped flight
disappears
in a gunmetal sky

An intracloud flash
brightens night like day

Thunder crashes—too close—
and yet
a ruby-throated hummer
darts
untroubled
even as a rush of wind
swings the feeder
in a wide-wider arc
on the porch

Rain begins to ping
then pelt the windows

In our log cabin
screen door left open
we lie content on quilted beds

inhale fresh air
and pine
the busyness we carried here
erased by the green fuse
of incipient summer—
receptive to woods and water
fire and air
our bodymind fills
with a buoyancy
that almost makes us giddy

Your arm across my belly
you turn and ask
What in the heck
have we been doing with our time?

The Bookmobile

Every two weeks, we'd search the horizon
for a distant cloud of dust. It never failed us.

Into the dry dirt lot the bookmobile rolled toward
a long line of small bodies baking in South Dakota heat.

Finally, finally, when the door to the trailer opened,
the bookmobile lady in wire-rimmed glasses appeared,

her face a text of perception. Black hair swept high on her head,
she stood in her crisp white blouse.

One by one, she handed us a towel to wipe sweaty hands
before allowing us to cross her threshold.

Inside, a fan blew cool air, and we felt it a holy place
so different from our homes.

I thumbed through pages of Scarlett O'Hara, but Nancy Drew proved
more exciting in her blue roadster—as did the flying flanks
of *The Black Stallion* and Flame, manes streaming free.

But it was Francie who changed my life.

Like the tree of heaven that sprouted between cracked cement
outside her Brooklyn tenement,

she encouraged me to push ever upward, to rise from my own dirt lot,
and to grow, grow green and alive.

Starry, Starry Night

for Vincent Van Gogh

At first I tried a sestina.
Aghast
Van Gogh burst through the rigid form
threw out formal end words
expanding
the vision
creating explosions
of a whir-swirling
ocher-orange world
spinning like stars
moon and sun
until his own fire radiated—
a celestial sphere
in the heavens

Following him into shimmering light
I unfurled my shadows
darkness touching a sky
alive and shining with stardust
until the glow absorbed the I
and we were out of time
out of mind
until nothing else mattered
but that cobalt-blue sky
and the floating
      floating
         floating

Winter Sunset

Naples, Florida

In the final moments of the sun's syzygy
with the moon and earth,
crowds of sunset watchers at seaside
begin to lower their voices.

The setting sun deceives as it disappears,
swells into a fireball.
Those with cameras rush to preserve
the day's finale on film.

In the moment when ocean swallows sun,
a man hammers on a brass gong
giving rise to vigorous applause. Like a cue,
conversation ascends to a higher pitch.

In the final symphonic movement,
a green flash can appear.
Most people hope to experience it
once in a lifetime.

Lovers stroll barefoot along the beach
in the deepening glow with clasped hands.
Sandpipers line up along the shoreline,
the entire length of the sand's subtle curve.

Often when the air echoes with celebration,
the murmuration of thousands of sea crows begins
to wing its way across the Gulf. As they come
closer, one can hear the rustle of wings,

how they loop back upon themselves—
wheeling, diving—
a black velvet ribbon rising,
falling,

this aerial choreography set against a sky
transformed to feathers of peach-pink-orchid.
Estuaries capture the muted colors
in liquid reflection.

Now egrets begin their journey north
along with white ropey lines of ibis.
The crescent moon lights an invisible
ladder rung by rung in the afterglow.

A song, a hundred songs, shape the air
from trees, and the voices of night begin
to commingle with the voices of day.
As breezes settle and day birds roost,

as moon, stars, and constellations
become the night light of the sleeping world,
another world begins.

In the Labyrinth of Old Love

with respect to Jim Simmerman, *The Last Word*

You can be the sun's fierce fire
if I can be the rainbow that links both land and sea.

You can be the obsidian flit and frit of volcanoes
if I can be the sea glass held within a child's hand.

You can be fall's harvest of leaves
if I can be the ashes piled against our roses.

You can be the river's constellation of stars
while I can be the swirling nebula.

You can be flame that tears its way through fields
if I can be charred ghosts of old melodies.

The burning bush of Moses, you can be that too,
and I'll be embers that sustain our hearth.

What We Didn't Lose

Steeped in the fragrance of sky, color pulls us
from recovery's blank corners.
We'd lost our way veiled in clouds
darkened by mist,
sleeping our mornings away.
Too tired, we'd say, and roll over, *too hard.*

An early doctor appointment opened time
and the hollows within the long night of our lives.
It had been nearly a year when that morning
greeted us with a white moon, beautiful, unspent,
scent of fresh earth, tiny mirrors of dew,

streets energized by walkers, joggers, bikes.
My husband and I, like Rip Van Winkles, became alert
to all we'd missed, the incidental bits and pieces
of the world's music, even an airplane shirring the air.
Look at the clouds, he said—*all the animals.*

Afterward, we took a tram to the beach. A few people
sat at tables in quiet conversation. Others, feet propped
on the railing, sipped coffee. A hush hovered
like sacred silence over the Gulf. We breathed in sea,
brine and fish, watched terns, skimmers, and gulls.

Though the physical limits of our lives have been redrawn,
air wraps us in light. I walk to his side, happy
for respite in uncertainty.
Draping my arms around him, he reaches
for my hands.

Notes

"Woman Wrapped in Orange" was written for my daughter, Maribeth, who after her nephew Sam died, celebrated his life in orange.

"1929" was written for my grandmother, who sold Dermetics during the Depression to keep her home together.

The boys mentioned in "Dealing With the Dead," Zach and Sam, are my grandchildren. They died at ages 7 and 15 from mitochondrial disease.

The sequence of poems "What You Left Me," "Angel Flying Too Close to the Ground," "Shifting Sands at Bonita Beach," and "In the Shortened Days of December" were written for my father, Wayne Horton.

"Improv on Blue" was written after a concert at Carnegie Hall by my son, David Cieri.

Acknowledgments

An Ariel Anthology: "Along the Fox River," "Waiting for the Light Rail"

The Aurorean: "Veterans Day"

Avocet: "Praise" (titled "Late December Sun")

Blue Heron Review: "All There's Left to Say"

The Centrifugal Eye: "What You Left Me," "Rocky III"

Crab Creek Review: "Improv on Blue"

Dreams and Secrets Anthology: "Losing Language"

Ekphrastic Review: "Gabriele Münter Paints Her Lover"

Five Willows Press: "Boating on the Yerres"

Frogpond Journal: the untitled opening haiku

Good Works Review: "How Light Casts Its Net"

Journal of Modern Poetry: "Winter Sunset"

Kentucky Review: "Renoir Paints My Husband and Me at Breakfast in Cagnes-Sur-Mer"

Peninsula Pulse: "Skipping Stones in Ireland

Persimmon Tree—Central States: "Dear Vincent"

Poetry East: "In the Labyrinth of Old Love"

Poetry That Moves: "Maybe"

Portage Magazine: "Backpacking in North Central Wisconsin"

Quill and Parchment: "On the 14th Anniversary of Her Death," "Angel Flying Too Close to the Ground"

Red Cedar Review: "Woman Wrapped in Orange"

Red-Headed Stepchild: "Shifting Sands at Bonita Beach"

Spindrift Magazine: "How to Deal with the Dead"

Tiger's Eye Press: "Regret Nothing," "In the Days When Wood Was Unaffordable"

VerseWright: "At a Writer's Retreat in the North Woods of Wisconsin"

Windhover: "I Say Yes" (titled "Touched by the Sacred")

Your Daily Poem: "Woman Wrapped in Orange," "Skipping Stones in Ireland," "On the Fourteenth Anniversary of My Mother's Death," "The Bookmobile" (titled "South Dakota Summer")

Awards: "Skipping Stones in Ireland," honorable mention, Peninsula Pulse Hal Contest; "Without a Voice" (2nd place) and "Ripple" (3rd place), 2017 Jade Ring Contest; "Boating on the Yerres," 1st place, 2014 Peace Award, Florida State Poets Association.

"Maybe" was featured the month of December, 2015, on the North Shore Pace buses operating between Evanston and Highland Park, as well as from Highland Park north to Waukegan.

"Along the Fox River" and "Winter Sunset" were nominated for a Pushcart.

I would like to express many thanks and appreciation to my daughter, Maribeth, who encouraged me and made many helpful comments from the manuscript's inception and throughout; to Sarah Sadie, founder of Odonata Creative, where people find time and space to achieve creative break-throughs and bloom; to Patt Clark and Rebecca Evans for their very helpful critiques; to F. J. Bergmann for her technological expertise in formatting; to Margaret Rozga and The Poetry People; to ISPS Writer's Group (Wilda Morris, Michael Escoubas, Barbara Robinette, and Candace Armstrong); to Kathie Giorgio of AllWriters Studio in Waukesha, WI; to Grace River Poets Anjie Kokan and Liz Rhodebeck for our shared goals all these years; and to the poets who read *Still* and wrote blurbs. Finally, a special thank you to FutureCycle Press and my editor, Diane Kistner, for her dedication to making this book the best it could be. Diane made every aspect of the publishing process one of the most enjoyable journeys I've experienced.

About FutureCycle Press

FutureCycle Press is dedicated to publishing lasting English-language poetry books, chapbooks, and anthologies in both print-on-demand and Kindle formats. Founded in 2007 by long-time independent editor/publishers and partners Diane Kistner and Robert S. King, the press incorporated as a non-profit in 2012. A number of our editors are distinguished poets and writers in their own right, and we have been actively involved in the small press movement going back to the early seventies.

The FutureCycle Poetry Book Prize and honorarium is awarded annually for the best full-length volume of poetry we publish in a calendar year. Introduced in 2013, our Good Works projects are anthologies devoted to issues of universal significance, with all proceeds donated to a related worthy cause. Our Selected Poems series highlights contemporary poets with a substantial body of work to their credit; with this series we strive to resurrect work that has had limited distribution and is now out of print.

We are dedicated to giving all of the authors we publish the care their work deserves, making our catalog of titles the most diverse and distinguished it can be, and paying forward any earnings to fund more great books.

We've learned a few things about independent publishing over the years. We've also evolved a unique, resilient publishing model that allows us to focus mainly on vetting and preserving for posterity poetry collections of exceptional quality without becoming overwhelmed with bookkeeping and mailing, fundraising, or taxing editorial and production "bubbles." To find out more about what we are doing, come see us at www.futurecycle.org.

The FutureCycle Poetry Book Prize

All full-length volumes of poetry published by FutureCycle Press in a given calendar year are considered for the annual FutureCycle Poetry Book Prize. This allows us to consider each submission on its own merits, outside of the context of a contest. Too, the judges see the finished book, which will have benefitted from the beautiful book design and strong editorial gloss we are famous for.

The book ranked the best in judging is announced as the prize-winner in the subsequent year. There is no fixed monetary award; instead, the winning poet receives an honorarium of 20% of the total net royalties from all poetry books and chapbooks the press sold online in the year the winning book was published. The winner is also accorded the honor of being on the panel of judges for the next year's competition; all judges receive copies of all contending books to keep for their personal library.

Made in the USA
Lexington, KY
30 September 2018